202
TURTLE HAIKU

THE STORY OF PONG

BY

ESTHER B. JIMENEZ

authorHOUSE®

AuthorHouse™
1663 Liberty Drive
Bloomington, IN 47403
www.authorhouse.com
Phone: 1-800-839-8640

First published by AuthorHouse   12/02/2011

ISBN: 978-1-4670-6214-5 (sc)

Printed in the United States of America

My sincere acknowledgement for the support and effort of Amy Reeves.

This book is printed on acid-free paper.

CONTENTS

DEDICATION VII

PREFACE IX

FOREWORD XIII

ACKNOWLEDGEMENTS XV

ABOUT THE AUTHOR XVII

REVIEWS FROM XIX

CHAPTER 1 Meeting A New Friend 1

CHAPTER 2 Giving A Name 2

CHAPTER 3 Welcome Pong 3

CHAPTER 4 A Memorable Day 4

CHAPTER 5 New Habitat 5

CHAPTER 6 Turtle Information 6

CHAPTER 7 Unique Behavior 8

CHAPTER 8 The Feeling Is mutual 10

CHAPTER 9 A Companion 11

CHAPTER 10 Still Searching 13

CHAPTER 11 Separation Anxiety 14

CHAPTER 12 Turtle Club 16

CHAPTER 13 More Of Us 17

CHAPTER 14 Mysterious Turtle 19

CHAPTER 15 Show Time 21

CHAPTER 16 Socialization 33

CHAPTER 17 Surprise Performance 34

CHAPTER 18 Extended Family 35

CHAPTER 19 Adoption 37

CHAPTER 20 Pong's Conversation With The Gang 39

CHAPTER 21 Till Next Time 42

SOME FACTS ABOUT WATER/AQUATIC TURTLES 44
MESSAGE FROM THE AUTHOR 48
TURTLES 50
ACRONYMS 52
A PRAYER FOR ANIMALS AND PETS 53
MY DREAMS OF TURTLES 54
"THAT'S ME PONG" 55
PONG'S CIRCLE OF FRIENDS 57

DEDICATION

For PONG, Ning, Jing, Mong, Haver,
Donna, Tello, Hanzel, Gretel, Jezzebel,
Polka, Ninja, Kwitib, Bubwit, Munger,
Terra, Apollo, Ping^2, Bong, Bing, Prince,
Ting, Lazy, Jill, Jack, Juliet, Romeo,
Delilah, Samson, Pilar, Pepe, Elmer,
Clancy, Bubbles, Squirt, Nala and Simba.
These TURTLES are significant in my
life. They are my nephews', nieces',
friends', my own turtles and even stray
and adopted ones.

PREFACE

"Why 202 Turtle Haiku?", you may ask. Or where did I get
this title?"
First, let me start explaining what Haiku is, for those who
don't know.
Mr. Webster says, "it is an unrhymed verse form of Japanese
origin having three lines usually 5, 7 and 5 syllables
respectively."
So it is a traditional form of Japanese poetry consisting of
five beats in the first line, seven in the second and five in
the third.
Haikus are usually about nature but you can choose whatever
subject you'd like to focus on.
I chose Turtle Haiku because of my turtle pet named, "Pong."
This haiku is about him and the rest of the turtle gang.
I am not a Haiku poet, but I am just overwhelmed to write
Pong's story in a haiku manner 5,7 and 5 syllable three lines.
I was writing the Turtle Haiku until I reached the 101 plus haiku
when my nephew Francis John suggested to make it 202, doubling
the 101 for a change.
101 is the number that is frequently referred to as titles like 101
Elephant Jokes, 101 Cleaning Tips, 101 Quotations, 101 Riddles
and many more.
Since I have already written more than 101 Haikus, why not
continue up to 202, right? So, "202 Turtle Haiku" is the
official title of my book. And I like the sound too, very rhythmic.
Actually it is more than 202, including Pong's own poem, the
author's message and some facts about water and aquatic turtles.
Since some reviewers of Pong's story requested for his pictures, I
thought of inserting few of them at the center fold of the book.

Pong participated in this Haiku poetry. Portion of the poetry came from his observation around him including me.
I tried to make it a real talking turtle through instilling my thoughts and imaginations in Pong's image. I tried to give life to his story.

I have learned a lot from taking care of Pong and my other turtles. If people would pay more attention to some animal behaviors, like my pet Pong, they could learn some virtues.

Turtles are persistent, patient and with a lot of perseverance. These, I have observed when Pong tried to climb up persistently and able to reach his target place. And this is a sign of a positive attitude.
Turtles are cautious, confident and with a lot of courage. When I placed Pong on a higher counter, he didn't want to continue walking, knowing it would be dangerous if he did. Once he learned that it was safe to go on, then he was confident to do it, not only once but many times.
As a hatchling, Pong already showed a sign of courage, swimming at distance towards us. He also showed independence, getting away from the other hatchlings and from his mother.
Another virtue is Pong's natural resiliency. He is strong, as evidenced by carrying a heavy load on his back. It's not only Pong with physical trait like this, all turtles I guess.

How about the famous slogan, "Slow But Sure?"
I witnessed that too, when Pong started to walk slowly, progressing to walking fast.
I know it's worth to mention their virtues and I indeed learned from Pong through my close observation of his unique behaviors. Most part of the haiku is Pong's dialogue and often times he addresses me as his mom, rescuer and master. I don't mind even mother turtle, turtle lover or trainer is totally acceptable.

PONG'S HAIKU FOREWORD

"I am slow but sure
Cautious, persistent and strong
With tricks of my own."

FOREWORD

I must admit this is the first time I read A haiku-formatted poetry.
As I was reading the entire book, I found myself counting the
"5-7-5" format with my fingers. I'm amazed at how Esther was able
to write these many Haikus and at the same time tells a story of her
favorite pet turtle, "PONG."
What I learned from this book is "friendship." It is a friendship that
is built on trust, caring, compassion, and unconditional love for each
other.

Not only that this poetry has a story, it is also informational.
I learned facts about turtles in a fun-loving manner. My two kids,
whom I also read this book to, thought the fact about "turtles
can also breathe from the rear end," funny and yet factual.

My son MJ, who is 9 years old shares this comment about the book,
"I love it because it has feelings and I cried when Pong said that
Apollo is his "bro." It was emotional for me."
*Note: He was referring to Chapter 18, "Extended Family." In
addition, Apollo is our pet turtle whom I rescued from being
smashed by passing cars.*

As for Miranda, my daughter who is 7 years old, this is her comment
about the book, "It is really good because it's telling about turtles
and how Pong and Tita became friends."

On behalf of my family, we are privileged to read your book and
share our thoughts with you. My kids and I do agree that your love
for these wonderful creatures is infectious. We are privileged to have
witnessed the caring thoughts and love for Pong first—hand.

Your love for turtles is contagious, that when we drive around where there's a possibility of turtle habitat, we look for any turtle(s) to rescue.
My kids find it hard to resist borrowing books about turtles, most especially MJ, a strong proponent of endangered turtles/tortoise.
He gets sad and mad when he sees turtles being hurt on TV.

Last but not the least, when we do rescue another turtle, we know whom to call. My kids will call out to their Tita Esther, whom they named, the "Turtle Expert."

Monalisa G. Bernabe
(Computer Engineer)
A mother of two beautiful kids,
MJ and Miranda.

ACKNOWLEDGEMENTS

My sincere thanks to:

. . . my nephew Francis John who has helped me
putting this book together, with his interesting
suggestions. His poem about turtles is one of his
contributions.
. . . all turtles or tortoise especially Pong and the rest
of the gang, (Esther's turtle team) who were
created by GOD for us to imitate their virtues.
. . . all turtle lovers who give extra attention to one of
the beautiful creatures on earth.
. . . Dr. Brazelton, the vet who took care of Pong when
he was very ill.
. . . The Anti-Cruelty Society, who continuously are
receiving abandoned and abused animals including
reptiles like the turtles.
. . . the Chicago Turtle Club members, who diligently
hold meetings to discuss different topics regarding
turtles and tortoise, educating members and non-
members about hatchlings, turtle cares, man-made
habitats and more.
. . . my parents, sister, brothers, in-laws, some relatives
(especially Beth who helps me take care of the turtles)
and friends who tolerate my craziness about turtles
and learn to enjoy them as well.
. . . my nephews, nieces and grandchildren, who also are
pet lovers and have turtles of their own.
. . . the people who did review my book, who stopped
from their routine task just to read the manuscript, and

to my friend Monalisa and her two kids(MJ and Miranda) for their feedback.

. . . But most of all to our Creator who created all of us including these unique, beautiful creatures.

ABOUT THE AUTHOR

Esther B. Jimenez is a native of Manila, Philippines, a nurse
by profession, a US Citizen and residing in Illinois, USA.

She had published four books:
"365 Days Food For Thoughts," "Bible Tidbits," "What's In
My Heart? Volume I, and What's In My Heart? Volume II,
(a collection of poems and poetry from the author's heart.)

She is one of the contributors/authors of the famous book,
"Cup Of Comfort Devotional," with two short articles for
August 3rd and August 16th.

Another book is already being processed for publishing
and coming out very soon, ("Have Phun With Elefants.")
It's about elephant jokes, riddles and knock-knock games.

"Gather Around The Table"(Prayers at meal time) is next to
this book.

Esther is a member of Author's Marketing Group in Illinois,
a member of Chicago Turtle Club.
A columnist of Via Times, a Newsmagazine catered to
Asian-American community in Chicago.
Esther reads and writes a lot and paints sceneries and nature.

Obviously, she is a pet lover, used to have two dogs and two

cats. Now she has Pong and other turtles and a Shih Tzu dog named, "Benjie."
She rescues abandoned and stray animals, especially turtles crossing the road.

REVIEWS FROM . . .

I really enjoy reading poetry in Haiku format. The cover art is quite nice although I especially like the picture of Pong on the back cover. The story itself is interesting. Thank you for sharing Pong's story

Laura Brazelton, DVM

The story of Pong and his tank mates are inspiring and enjoyable to read. But it's more than that. Through the use of artfully selected lines you can see GOD's beauty in nature and the author alike. You will definitely want to meet Pong and his owner after you read this collection of Haikus.

Ted Campbell
President of T.A.R.A.H.
(The Alliance of Reptile and
Amphibian Hobbiyists)

Charming, narrative from Pong who expresses very sweetly of his life playmates. I learned quite a bit about water turtles. If you had pictures (or drawings) of Pong and his life, I think they would add beauty to the book. Perhaps you could write about part II of his further adventure.

Gail Watson
Newsletter Coordinator,
Secretary of T.A.R.A.H.

Esther B. Jimenez

What a sweet, gentle, delightful book! This book is not only recommended for children but for adults too, especially for all turtle lovers. I enjoy reading it.

Sam Leikin
A teacher from
Peacock Middle School

I enjoyed so much the story of Pong. I like how you describe his personality. I hope people will read this book for they would learn about turtles, that they are unique and interesting.
I do appreciate that you included that "baby turtles can make it" and very independent as soon as they see the outside world. Indeed, they are very delicate creatures even though they are so prehistoric and tough looking.
Each turtle can be very attached to their owners (like when Esther went on vacation, Pong was very much affected.)
Some turtles are not social, some turtles behave well, and some are docile. It is obvious that Pong has had quite an impact. I think it would be wonderful if turtle/tortoise owners would take time to get to know these fine reptiles and have grown to love them as I have.
Thank you for sharing this with me.

Michelle Storck
Jim's Pet Shop
Addison, Illinois

First of all thank you for including Bubbles and Squirt in your "Dedication." I really like the book especially the facts about them. When Pong asked if people want to see his baby scales, I would like to answer yes.
I am wondering if you are going to add pictures of Pong, it would look cute though. These are only my thoughts.
I am amazed and enjoy reading the book.
How could you come up with so many haikus?
the book is interesting and I read it non-stop. I love it with no hesitation. Thank you for everything Tita.

Bea C.
Youth For CHRIST

CHAPTER 1 Meeting A New Friend

My brother and I
Were at the small lake one time
Saw a small turtle.

A baby turtle
With orange belly color
Size of a teaspoon.

My brother scooped him
From the edge of the water
Gently with his hand.

The small lake has flocks
Of mallards and geese, maybe
Big fish underneath?

These predators can
Intimidate these little
Fellows called turtles.

I say, we saved this
Creature from the claws of the
(Vultures), predators.

This is the real start
Of a bright future friendship
With a reptile friend.

CHAPTER 2 Giving A Name

Indeed, he is cute
"What name shall we give?", I asked.
My brother answered,

"Pong" it is, sounds good,
From then on we called him "Pong,"
A painted turtle.

Sweet name for a pet
A turtle deserves a name,
Like everyone else.

I presumed he is
A male, so where did we get
His name? Here it is.

In our country the
Philippines, there's a cartoon
Character named Pong,

Mind you it is a
Turtle, and the word turtle
Translates to "pagong,"

Didn't you notice, the
Rhyme it gives? sounds Pong Pagong
So Pong, it is, yes!

CHAPTER 3 Welcome Pong

Nobody at home
Knew about the habitat
Of the small turtles.

But still we welcome
Pong with care and compassion.
Welcome tiny Pong!

We started talking
To him and letting him feel
We care about him.

I can't explain this
Excitement I have, seeing
Him swimming, splashing.

My first time to see
A colored/painted turtle
And swims so funny.

Right at that moment
I claimed this beautiful pet
As my own to keep.

How is it to have
And keep a water turtle?
We'll know later, right?

CHAPTER 4 A Memorable Day

Memorable Day
Two years ago, month of May
It's on the eighth day.

My first time to have
A turtle pet, I was thrilled
I will remember

This important day
Owning a beautiful pet,
Reptile pet, my Pong.

I fell in love at
First sight, holding him in my
Palm, cute little one.

Every time I go
To the place where we saw Pong
I can't help but smile.

Now, Pong is well grown
Yet still small, but know him more
Our friendship is great.

You'll learn more, you'll see
Flip the pages and read more
About my pet Pong.

CHAPTER 5 New Habitat

Away from the lake
To the contained tap water
On a glass round bowl.

First food was lettuce
Toothless Pong he just nibbled
Bite marks in the green.

Only improvised
The aquarium that Pong used
Has tiny gray rocks.

A lamp light he needs
To bask himself and relax
A new habitat.

I'm sure Pong feels strange
In a new environment
Real big adjustment.

He'll be used to hear
People talking all the time
That's new to my Pong.

Pong will adjust well
He seems happy and playful
Habitat, real new.

CHAPTER 6 Turtle Information

Pong is talking to the readers

What is that floating?
Ooops! I'm shedding, it's part of
The Reptile culture.

I am a reptile
We do shed from time to time
My mom collects them.

She puts them in a
Nice box, do you want to see
My first baby scales?

How about this, I
Can only have meals in the
Water, plain as that.

I can also breath
Through my rear end, no kidding
That's us, the turtles.

My back looks stone rock
But I'm sensitive inside
So take care of me.

Otherwise, it'll hurt
If someone touch my back hard
Handle me gently.

I have a secret
To share: "We don't have vocal
Chords, no sound, just hiss."

<u>CHAPTER 7 Unique Behavior</u>

Pong's human mother and himself telling story

Pong likes to listen
Knows my voice and likes its sound
Very smart turtle.

He does swims a lot
Splash, splash, the sound he creates
It means "look at me,

And see my new tricks,
I can poke this glass, like birds
With my beak-like mouth."

My master spoils me
Feeding me with small minnows
Salad on the side.

One trick I can show
Is, to distinguish the food;
I know the color

Of the bottle cap,
The yellow I want, green no
Dried shrimps, it's the best.

Walk, walk, walk, that's me
Pong, strolling in the carpet
Good exercise, huh!

Months have gone so fast
I'm now a tablespoon size
And with stronger splash.

<u>CHAPTER 8 The Feeling Is mutual</u>

Pong expresses his feelings

I see my master
Happy and glad, the feeling
Is mutual, indeed.

She rescued me from
The lake, I was by myself
I'm very thankful.

She really takes care
Of me, hums and sings for me
Like a lullaby.

I sleep on her chest
Not even moving around
I can feel her love.

Oh, I am lucky
I found a caring mommy
Treats me humanly.

I wish I could do
Something to return the love
She gives genuinely.

Aha! Let me think
I have a surprise for her
So, flip the pages.

CHAPTER 9 A Companion

Pong is lonely

Do I need someone?
Tortoise or a fish? Turtle?
My mommy thinks so.

She tried to find one
Bought a female painted, too
From Florida state.

By the way, I am
A male turtle, according
To the nature book.

"Ping" is the name of
The turtle from Florida,
And she is cute too.

But she seemed depressed
Maybe because of her trip
Via air cargo.

Ping didn't stay longer
She died in few weeks, it's sad
My mom was sad too.

Will I ever have
A companion in the near
Future, I wonder?

I don't know if I
Need a companion, it seems
I can live alone.

Another few months
Have gone, and my master tried
To look for turtles.

Aha! a pair came
Two baby turtles, sliders
We're not the same kind.

Every new comer
Has different containers
Me, in the same bowl.

The pair didn't last long
Nature took them, died as well.
Good-bye again, friends.

Again, they have names
"Bong" and "Bing," female and male
Beautiful turtles.

CHAPTER 10 Still Searching

My mommy's friend asked
For a turtle, she bought one
A bigger slider.

But few months after
The slider was returned back
To my sweet mommy.

By the way his name
Is "Mong," the biggest of all
Turtles in our home.

Two of us now in
A separate container
Painted and slider.

Let's pause a moment
To tell you that this Haiku
Is about me, Pong,

About some turtles
In my life and the love of
My master for us.

It's me now who tells
The story about me and
The gang, the turtles.

CHAPTER 11 Separation Anxiety

Pong's Gripes

My master went for
A three week vacation and
Beth took care of me.

I was sad, depressed
Didn't eat and I was sluggish
I missed her so much.

By the time she's back
Time I need to see a vet
My master was sad.

She cried, shed her tears
I need to get well, I fought
I need my master.

Back to normal me
Motile, splash heard again and
Smile I see in her.

The vet's instructions
Are to feed me with minnows
Lettuce, and spinach.

At first, I ignored
The fish minnows and guppies
Then I used my skill.

Hunting I was good
Chasing the other swimmers
My strength was regained.

Anxiety gone
No vacation and she is
Here with me again.

Note from Pong's human mom

Pets and animals
Have compassion too, indeed
Pong proves it to me

CHAPTER 12 Turtle Club

My mommy found a
Flyer in the vet clinic
It says, "Turtle Club"

Chicago Turtle
Club, it is, for all turtle
And Tortoise lovers.

My sweet mommy joined
The club meeting, one Sunday
Met turtle lovers.

From then on, she has
Been informed and updated
Of the news events.

On one occasion
The members are requested
To bring their turtles.

My mom took me there
So with motile Ning and Jing
A real fellowship.

I love to be there
Have met different turtles
Enjoyed and had fun.

CHAPTER 13 More Of Us

Pong still conversing

You have read about
Ping, Bong, Bing and Mong, it seems
Pretty good buddies,

Mong, a cute slider
Is the only survivor
The rests are painted.

She found another
Scoopful size painted turtle
Very cute named Prince.

Prince stayed with the rests
For at least five weeks and then
He expired, it hurts.

One member of the
Club sold one of his painted
A dollar coin size.

Cute too, named her Ning
But with a tiny bump on
Her left cheek, poor Ning.

Three weeks after that
My rescuer went to a
Reptile Swap Market.

Guess what? another
Beautiful, painted turtle
And she named her "Jing."

Now we are in four
Different bowl containers
With our floating toys.

So the routine goes
Feeding, bathing, basking and
Walking here and there.

The turtles mentioned
In the Dedication page
Are significant.

At the last pages
My mom will identify
Each of the turtles.

What a life we have
What's next? Aha! another
Interesting thing.

In the next chapter
Is very interesting
Stand-by dear readers.

CHAPTER 14 Mysterious Turtle

Story of a new member

Amazing event,
One day when my mom came home
Saw in the driveway

A painted turtle
Not moving, seemed basking and
Bigger than myself.

My mom thought it was
Me who might have escaped and
Just waiting for her.

It was mysterious
And questions arise on how,
Where and who owns her?

One opinion is,
"A friend dropped her" another
Says, "Comes from the pond."

Is it one of GOD's
Wonders of wonder, maybe!
Did she hear, splashes?

From a distance far?
Maybe she knew that there are
Four turtles at home.

More opinions, more
Guesses, but the bottom line
GOD sent her to us.

A unique name was
Given to her, "Haver" from
The street Haver Hill.

It's the address in
Which I live and the rest of
The gang, the turtles.

Now we're family
Me (Pong), Mong, Ning, Jing and the
Newcomer, Haver.

Quite a story, for
A water turtle like me,
With human feelings.

<u>Chapter 15 Show Time</u>

I really love my
Human mommy just because
She speaks our language.

She not only found
A turtle family but
Buys turtle stuff too.

In one Chicago
Turtle Club meeting, the gang
And me, Pong showed off.

I pretended that
I understood my master
By moving my neck,

Right to left, left to
Right and I poked the glass and
Act as a sweet bird.

Ning and Jing were there
Mong stayed home, felt out of place
With these three turtles.

They think I am smart
I think I'm a unique pet
I love to show off.

HERE ARE SOME OF
PONG'S PICTORIALS.

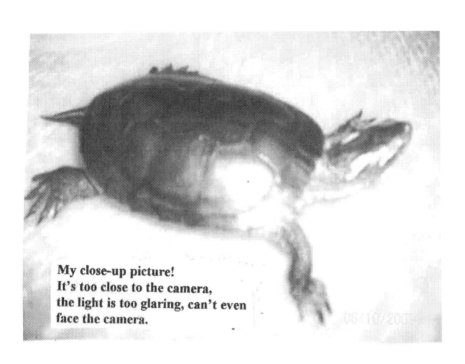

My close-up picture!
It's too close to the camera,
the light is too glaring, can't even
face the camera.

Me and PONG at the Blessing of the Pets,   October 4, 2009

Beth, Pong and Benjie at the Blessing of the Pets. October 4, 2009

Me and PONG at the Blessing of the Pets,   October 4, 2009

GREEN CAP COVER

YELLOW CAP COVER

I can see my food from here. Too bad this picture is black and white.
I like the one with yellow cap cover.
It's shrimp yummy, yummy!

I just had my shower.
Can someone hand me that green towel?
Ooops! I forgot, this is a black and white picture.
Ok, I need that towel with the flower design. Thanks!

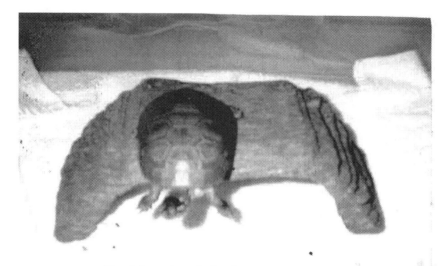

Basking time! Is that my shadow?

I am here at Twinsburg, Ohio basking
and enjoying my uncles' garden.

This is how to escape.

Do you need help Ning?
How is the bump on your cheek?

Do you want to see my Jackson's moonwalk?

OR

Do you want to see my Travolta move?.

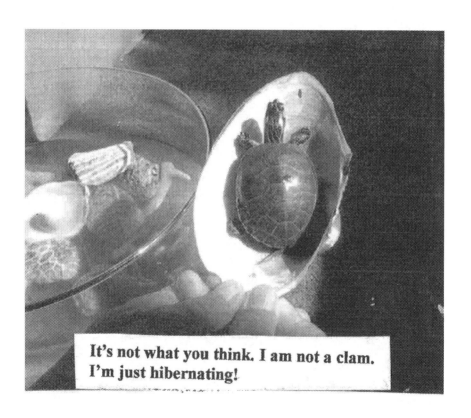

It's not what you think. I am not a clam. I'm just hibernating!

CHAPTER 16 Socialization

Sometimes the five of
Us are in one big bin with
Water for play time.

The people at home
Enjoy watching us splashing
Raising our small hands,

Looks like clapping our
Hands, chasing one another
Bumping together.

When water fitness
Is over, then basking takes
Place and I love it.

One thing you should know
Is our ways of showing our
Love for each other.

When you see us do
The nose to nose, that's love folks
Now you know, new thing.

Part of our culture
Is to bask on top of each
Other,(Unity?)

<u>Chapter 17 Surprise Performance</u>

Pong Got Talent

Our shells indeed are
Sensitive to touch I guess
We are ticklish, and

If someone will touch
Me at my back, It will look
Like I am dancing.

But one thing they don't
Know is I can really dance
One day when my mom

Was swaying her head
Side to side I did follow
Her by doing so;

I tiptoed back and
Forth, side to side and my mom
Indeed laugh so hard.

That was a real act
Dancing with her while she was
Humming melody.

This was my surprise
Performance for her, cha-cha
They did video me.

Chapter 18 Extended Family

A nine year old girl
Wished to have a turtle for
Christmas, and did ask

Santa for her gift
When my mom found out about
It, she surprised her,

With a pair, not one.
Delight and joy seen in her
Face with gratitude.

Beautiful name she
Gave to the pair, Bubbles and
Squirt, slider their kind.

See! I have my new
Extended family, what
A life I have, great!

Another story
Of extended family
A stray turtle, yes,

My mom's friend has him
She saved him from being smashed
That is Apollo!

Esther B. Jimenez

A Western painted
Turtle found crossing the street
With a shiny shell.

He is my buddy
My extended family
Welcome Apollo!

Chapter 19 Adoption

The original
Plan for the gift to that girl
Was this turtle from

The adoption place
"A painted about seven
Inches, heavyweight."

It's too big for a
Nine year old to have this as
A pet, so what's next?

To be honest I
Am scared of a big turtle
But what can I do?

As long as I won't
Get near her, it won't bother
Me at all, play fair!

I have heard her name
It's Terra, did I say it's
A she? Yes she is.

At this time, my mom
Is still looking for a good
Home, for big Terra.

So, attention all
Turtle lovers, adopt her
She'll be glad indeed.

Terra needs a home
Hopefully she can have one
Very soon, if not

My mom will keep her
For a while until she finds
The right home for her.

The right home is found
A lady from a small store
Asks to have Terra.

Good-bye friend Terra
Thank you for the time we spent
Be a good reptile.

Chapter 20 Pong's Conversation
With The Gang

In my own way, I
Know how to communicate
With my reptile friends.

I said good-bye to
Ping before she departed.
I sensed her good will.

When Mong came to my
Life, I told him he'll be back
Was I right? I was.

My little friends, the
Pair, were inseparable
I always see them

Holding hands at times;
They were not separated
Long, now both resting.

I was referring
To Bong and Bing, the sweetest
Small turtles ever.

I told Ning not to
Worry, for my mom will take
Care of her cheek bump.

I like her a lot
I feel like an older bro'
I'll look after her.

Jing and I have the
Same spot on our bellies, and
I told her maybe

We are related
Seemed to like that idea.
I also like Jing.

Haver is bigger
Than me, but she respects me
I respect her too.

Bubbles and Squirt are
Just acquaintances, they didn't
Stay long here with me.

About Terra, I'm
Glad she found a home, indeed
I'll truly miss her.

I see Apollo
Once in a while and that's fine
He's my older bro.

These are the turtles
I really see everyday
So let me start with,

Jezzebel, Munger,
Kwitib, Bubwit, Polka, Mong,
Jing, Ning, and Ninja.

Ooops! Haver, Hanzel,
Gretel, Donna and Tello
The rests don't live here.

<u>Chapter 21 Till Next Time</u>

The closing time is
Near, to end this book chapter;
This is the story

Of my life indeed
From my first existence to
The present event.

I look forward to
The second book of Haiku
The next episode.

Meantime, good-bye folks
See you next time at the part
Two of my story.

This is Pong, a sweet
Pet of Esther, the author
Of this turtle book.

I have a bookmark
Free for you, just ask my mom
She will give you some.

Haiku or not, is
The same thing because I am
Still the same turtle.

I love you all, but
I love my mom most of all,
Thanks for saving me.

SOME FACTS ABOUT WATER/AQUATIC TURTLES

(Some Facts about Painted Turtles)

That water turtles
Can only be fed in the
Water while they swim.

Turtles don't have teeth
Their hard beaks allow them to
Chew the food slowly.

They can hold their breath
For a long time, their tongues are
Fixed, that' s why they can't

Swallow the food fast
Can't eat out of the water,
Indeed it makes sense.

Interesting to
Know these facts about turtles
Amazing species.

That they have web feet
Can also stay on the ground
As necessary.

The shell is made of
Bone and is connected to
The spine and their ribs.

They do love to bask
Spring, Summer, Fall and Winter
Make sure to have an

Artificial light
At home, a lamplight will do
Let them be happy.

There are many facts
About the water turtles
And the like, tortoise.

Read more about them
Be concern, be kind to all
Turtles and tortoise.

Painted turtles don't
Raise their young, the babies go
Their own way, elsewhere.

Painted ones live in
Permanent freshwater such
Habitats as ponds

Lakes, marshes, sloughs, creeks
Hibernate during Winter
In a dormant life.

Have you wondered where
Do these turtles live and go?
They spend in burrow,

Of their freshwater
Habitat in the soft mud
At its bottom place.

One interesting
Fact is that there are no sex
Gender in painted

Turtles, their sex is
Determined by external
Temperature, if

The nest is very
Warm, all the baby turtles
Will be sure females;

And if it is cold
Then the baby turtles will
Be males, I'm amazed.

On the other hand
Male painted is different
From the female one.

Males, generally
Are smaller than the females,
Have longer front claws

And with longer tails
With thicker, concave, plastrons
Use for their mating.

There is Eastern and
Western painted, and Midland
They are colorful.

Let me give you at
Least few turtle languages
One is "basking time,"

Where in the turtles
Exposed themselves and relax
Under the sunlight.

"Hibernate," to pass
The Winter in a dormant
Or inactive state,

With lowered heart rate
Metabolism as well.
Plastrons, carapace,

Scutes, Shells and claws are
Turtles' body parts, not to
Forget, the webbed feet.

Hatchlings, means hatched eggs
The baby turtles that laid
On soft mud or land.

The scientific
Name for Eastern Painted Is
"Chrysemys picta."

They can grow up to
Eight or nine inches long and
Stand out from other

Turtles because of
Their smooth, shiny, dark flattened
Shell, they're beautiful !

<u>MESSAGE FROM THE AUTHOR</u>

I am grateful for
The chance that was given to
Me, to take care of

Creatures like turtles
They are also GOD's wonders
Beautiful beings.

When Pong swam towards
Our direction, then I knew
He was meant for us.

"Pong Pagong" is an
Adorable pet, very
Sweet, my favorite.

I really love Pong
And I am inspired to write
A Haiku poetry

About him, I hope
That the readers will enjoy
Reading Pong's story.

Again, my sincere
Thanks to all pets, animals
And turtle lovers.

The next time you see
A turtle, tortoise crossing
The road, stop . . . your car,

And help him cross or
Pick-him up, you have a choice
Let someone adopt,

This curious creature
Or call the hot-line for the
Anti—Cruelty.

Always remember
Turtles have rights too to live
In this world, agreed?

Reading and knowing
More about turtles, makes me
Love Pong more and more.

I LOVE YOU ALL TURTLES
IN THIS WORLD

TURTLES

What are turtles?
Many don't know
for they only understand
that they are slow.

Chinese believed
that they are bad luck
No benefits from them
even fame nor a buck.

Some people paint their shells
For their own delight and joy
But they don't realize
That turtles are not toys.

Certain people cook them
for soups
And claim, it tastes good
What they're doing, is
mean and rude.

Turtles are defenseless
Their shells aren't that hard
They can also be broken
And turn into shard.

They also have feelings
Like all other pets,
They can show their love
But their lives are at stake.

And always remember
That they are one of GOD's
creations and they are
uniquely beautiful.

(For all the turtles around the world
especially Pong and our other turtles)

Francis John Angelo Jimenez
8th Grade F. E. Peacock Middle School

ACRONYMS

T—urtle, terrapin, tortoise, triple T's for tenacity.
U—nique behavior(that's Pong) and has tricks of his own.
R—eptile family, where he is classified, but I am his now.
T—ender, loving, care, that's what I give to him.
L—ovable Pong, that's my turtle, my favorite.
E—nlightening it is, the virtues we can cultivate.
S—hell, scutes, shed, I learned from taking care of my Pong.

*   *   *   *   *   *   *

H—ello, let's do the Haiku poetry!
A—mazing thoughts occur in poet's mind.
I—nspiring poetry focused on nature.
K—in to a free verse, but they're not.
U—niquely done with no rhyme.

A PRAYER FOR ANIMALS AND PETS

Thank you LORD for Your creations and creatures, for the pets and
animals in the world; May You protect these creatures from harm and
cruelty, from the unspeakable abuse and brutality. May You give them
good masters, and caregivers that deserve their loyalty.
May You bless them and their masters always. May You touch others
who have no compassion, that they may learn to be kind to all creatures.
LORD, I pray mostly for the people who have lost their pets, that You
may be with them in their grieving, until their moments of recovery and
complete healing. Please continue to grant us a good heart and love for
animals and pets. All this I pray in JESUS' name, Amen!

MY DREAMS OF TURTLES

When you have turtle pets, what do you expect? Of course they are included in your dreams. I dream of turtles often times. One time, I dreamed of turtles in different colors, swimming not in the aquarium, but on the ground level water. They looked like colorful flowers or butterflies, swimming, splashing. Another night, I dreamed of catching them with my bare hand, and I was overwhelmed by their multitudes. Then few nights ago, a small turtle accidentally jumped on the toilet bowl. I scooped him right away washed it shell with soap, then I realized that turtles are sensitive to chemicals, so I rinsed the shell with the running water longer than ever. There was one afternoon that I dreamed of painted turtles, swimming in small pond, and I was on the boat, catching them with my right hand and gently putting them back in the water, just like that. Last night my dream was a little weird. A group of water turtle swimming at the man-made pond. People are watching them when suddenly two big cats sat at the edge of the pond. There was a still moment(like a camera in a still position). It caught the scene of one of the cats mouthing the turtles. I thought for a while the cat bit the head of the turtles, but when the camera was rolling it was the turtle who snapped the ear of the cat, Ha!Ha! Ha! I laughed so hard in my dream. Well, till next dream, see you in turtle land.

"THAT'S ME PONG"

(Pong's Own Haiku)

Walk, walk, walk, that's me
Pong, exploring the world, don't
You know I carry,

Pretty heavy load?
I can look at you face to
Face and my better

Viewing is side to
Side, though I'm the slowest of
All creatures on earth.

I am persistent
Witty and patient and I
Am a climber, a

Thinker, achiever.
Splash, splash, splash, that's me taking
A bath and at the

Same time having my
Snack, I can only have my
Meals in the water.

Ooops! I have a name
My rescuer calls me Pong
She saved me from the

Claws of the vulture
Now I have grown into the
Size of a cell phone.

PONG'S CIRCLE OF FRIENDS

INTRODUCTION OF PONG'S FRIENDS

We'll start with PONG:
He is the alpha turtle. He is the dancing turtle. Of course this book is about him. Pong is a sweet turtle, but I have to admit, he is a bully. If you put him with other turtles, he would chase them and open his mouth pretending to snap them.

Mong . . . the only red ear slider among the turtles here. He is the one that stayed with my friend, but was returned back to me. He is a male and about 7 inches long.

Ping . . . painted turtle, 4 ½ inches long, and she was the one I ordered from Florida, but didn't stay longer because of stress and exhaustion from the trip (maybe.) She passed away. She could have been a perfect match for Pong.

Ning . . . this is the one with bump or lump on her left cheek. After seeing a vet and given a steroid shot, she grew big after few months, She is bigger than Pong now.

Jing . . . I got her from the Reptile Flea Market where I met the T.A.R.A.H group. I bought from a guy and he claimed that his girlfriend returned the painted turtle to him when they broke up. Poor Jing, (caught in between love quarrel) I am glad to have her. She is 4 ½ inches long.

Haver . . . a stray turtle who just showed up in our driveway. Everyone guessed where he came from. There were lots of guesses. The bottomline is, our Creator sent him to us. And I accepted him with open arms and since our street is Haver, I named him, "Haver."

Donna and Tello . . . They were together and being sold at the Reptile Flea Market. They're both painted turtles. At first I was planning to give them as gifts for a 10 year old boy, a grandson of a friend, but I thought of keeping them. But I gave him another pair of red ear sliders. They are about 4-5 inches long.

Hanzel and Gretel . . . they are Eastern painted and about 4 inches long. I got them from the Flea market and I bought them together, because the vendor was separating them and selling them separately. I couldn't stand seeing them separated so, I asked the vendor to sell them both to me.

Jezzebel . . . she came from the pet shop and she was just picked up by a passer-by and gave her to the pet shop. The pet shop owner asked me if I would like to have another turtle. Again, she is a painted turtle and about 8 inches long. I kept her for a while, and to my surprise she started laying eggs. She did lay at least 8 eggs and I tried to put them in an improvised incubator, but they didn't survive.
(This is one of the most exciting event in my life, taking care of a pregnant turtle.)

Polka . . . from its name, got polka dots (black round spots on her side,) a painted turtle about 5 3/4 inches long and heavy. I got her from a Spanish pet store, and there's only one left so I purchased her.

Ninja . . . is from the Reptile Flea Market and she was sold there by her previous owner. She is a painted turtle about 5 ½ inches long but with short tail. Ninja is like Pong very attentive. Everytime I hold her, she seems listening, she extends her neck longer, trying to reach me . . . Compared to a person's personality, I would say she is a meek turtle.

Kwitib and Bubwit . . . they are from the Reptile Flea Market, too. They are very closed to each other, but Kwitib grows faster than Bubwit. Kwitib is about 4 inches long and Bubwit is 3 ½ inches long.

Munger . . . is my only snapping turtle. I found him crossing the Munger Road, Bartlett, Illinois, and that's where I got her name. She was muddy and seemed hungry. From the time I got her, we've never seen her snapped. I always talk to her and she seems to be pretty behaved and a tamed snapping turtle. She is about 7 ½ inches long from head to tail.

Note: Snapping turtles have long necks and can't hide their heads inside the shell, that's why they snap. Snapping is their defense mechanism.

Terra . . . was the one that was adopted by a store owner. I got her from Adopt-A-Pet place. Someone put her at the door of the foundation center and the staff asked me if I could find a home for her. Fortunately I did. She is a painted turtle and about 8 inches long.

Elmer . . . is a red ear slider owned by Diane K. a member of Chicago Turtle Club. At first Diane thought Elmer was a male, but eventually she laid eggs and realized he was a she. She was bought last September of 1972 and just turned 39 this month. She is about 7 inches long.

Clancy . . . a painted turtle, about 8 inches long, owned by my cousin's co-worker named, Jan, who shares story of Clancy and Pong with each other. That's what I called Turtle Networking.

Bubbles and Squirt . . . a Christmas turtle gift to a 9 year old girl named, Bea. They are both red ear sliders and about 4 inches long.

Nala and Simba . . . The newest pair I've included in the turtle circle of friends. My friend just called me recently, asking me if I could give her one or two of my turtles and I have explained that I can't just give my turtles away. So I purchased a pair of red ear slider and I gave them to my friends, (a couple.) Their granddaughter was the one who named the turtles, from the Lion King characters.

Apollo . . . he was the one found crossing the street by my best friend. He is a Western painted turtle about 5 inches long with very shiny carapace. He was named Apollo, after the Apple Orchard Golf Course, where he was found.

<u>Bing and Bong</u> . . . the turtle pair that Pong is referring in his story. Pong described them as a sweet couple, that he caught holding hands most of the time. They were both red ear sliders about 3 ½ inches long, both came from the Reptile Flea Market.

<u>Prince and Ting</u> . . . were tiny painted turtles rescued from the lawn of a Nursing Home. They were cute turtles, but didn't live long.

<u>Lazy</u> . . . a painted turtle about 4 inches long and I almost kept her. Another friend asked for a turtle for her grandson.

<u>Jack, Jill, Romeo, Juliet, Samson, Delilah, Pepe and Pilar,</u> are all Red Ear Turtle Sliders, about 7 to 9 inches long and residents of the Philippines. My brother Ralph and his son Ralp Jr. are the ones taking care of them.

WE ARE MEMBERS OF PONG'S CLUB

We Are:

P—eople Lovers
O—bservant Turtles
N—on Harmful Creatures
G—ood House Pets